SCHOODLES

This is a Carlton book

Text, design and illustration
© Carlton Books Limited 2010

Art Director & Illustrator: Elle Ward
Executive Editor: Barry Timms
Creative Director: Clare Baggaley
Editorial Director: Jane Wilsher
Production: Claire Hayward

Published in 2010 by Carlton Books Limited
An imprint of the Carlton Publishing Group
20 Mortimer Street, London W1T 3JW

2 4 6 8 10 9 7 5 3

A catalogue record for this book is
available from the British Library.

ISBN: 978-1-84732-558-7

JFMAMJJ SOND/10/6509
Printed in Dongguan, China

SCHOODLES

CARLTON
BOOKS

Draw things in the spaces

Write on the dotted lines

Colour in the pictures

Try using stickers or cut-outs

Add your own funny details

Scrawl, scribble, go crazy -
it's fun to schoodle!

This book belongs to

..........Mia Tellero..........

at ....

.... school

Who's travelling on
the school bus today?

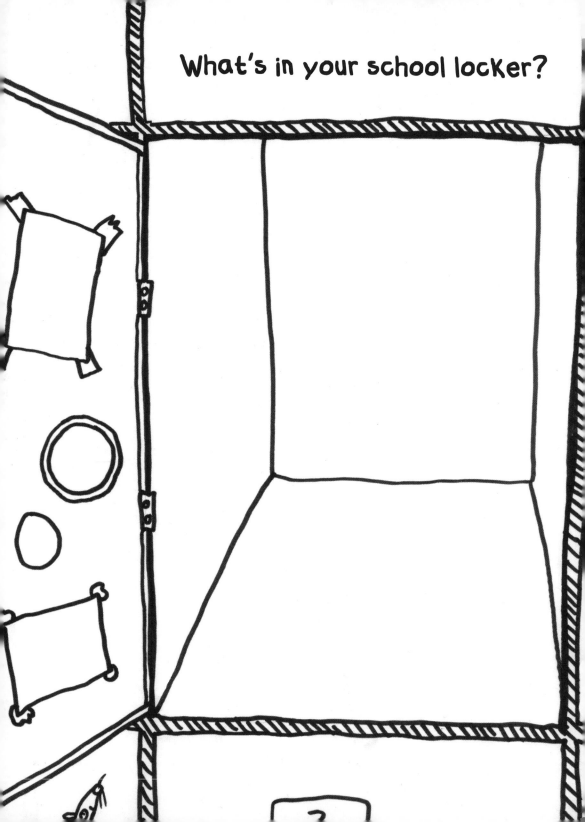

What's in your school locker?

Dig a tunnel to escape
from the classroom...

Bus, boat, train or UFO –
how will you get to school?

How high can you jump on the trampoline?

Give Lucy extra arms to
help her do her homework...

What has fallen into the school pond?

PROJECT 1: Draw the sounds
these instruments make...

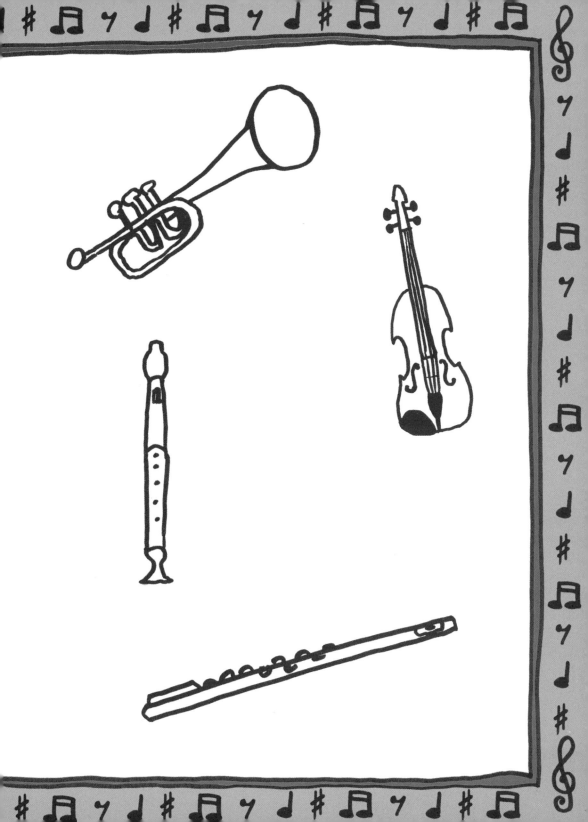

How long does your arm need to be to get the teacher's attention?

What pet do you keep in your pencil case?

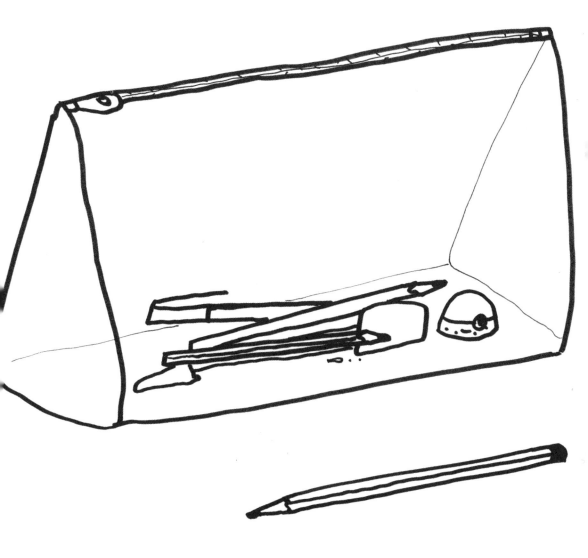

Finish off this homework machine...

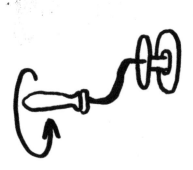

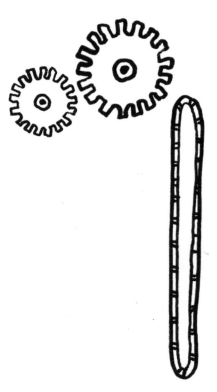

Practise your handwriting
by copying these styles:

lovely handwriting

lovely handwriting

lovely handwriting

lovely handwriting

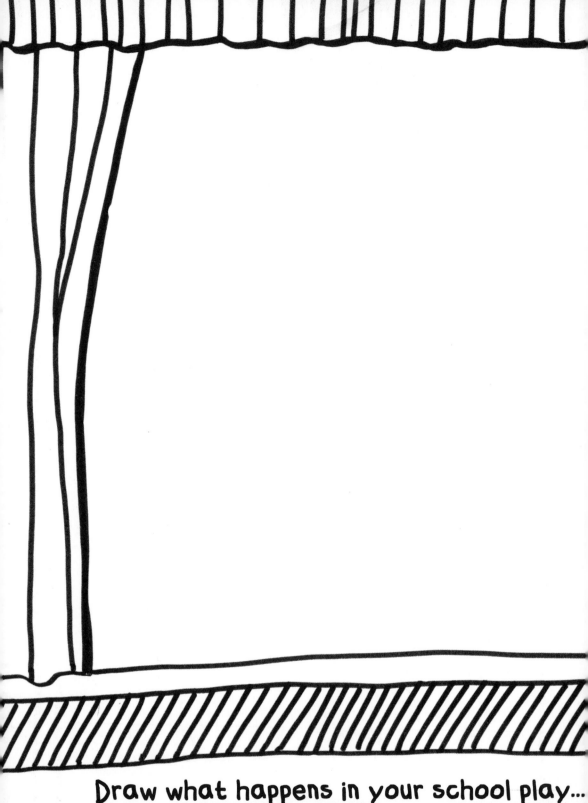

Draw what happens in your school play...

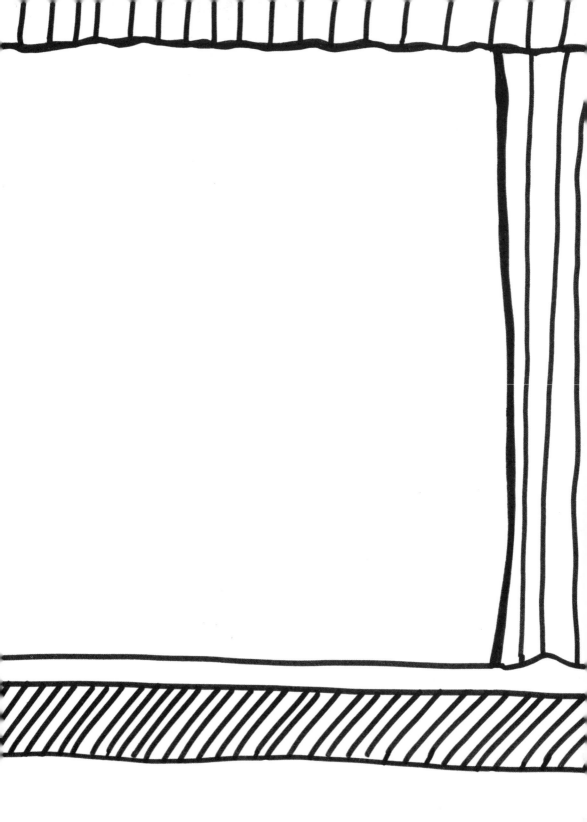

Take a school trip into outer space!

Awarded to:

....

For:

....

....

Who has won the school cup?

Draw how you've changed from years 1-4

Year 1

Year 2

Year 3

Year 4

What has crashed through
the classroom wall?

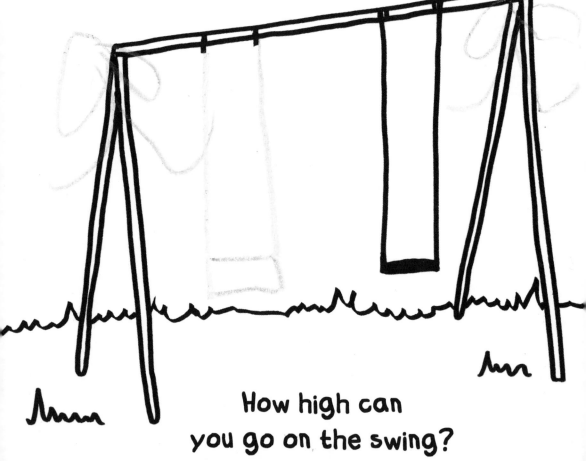

How high can
you go on the swing?

How many books do you think Gemma can carry?

Draw the view from the classroom window...

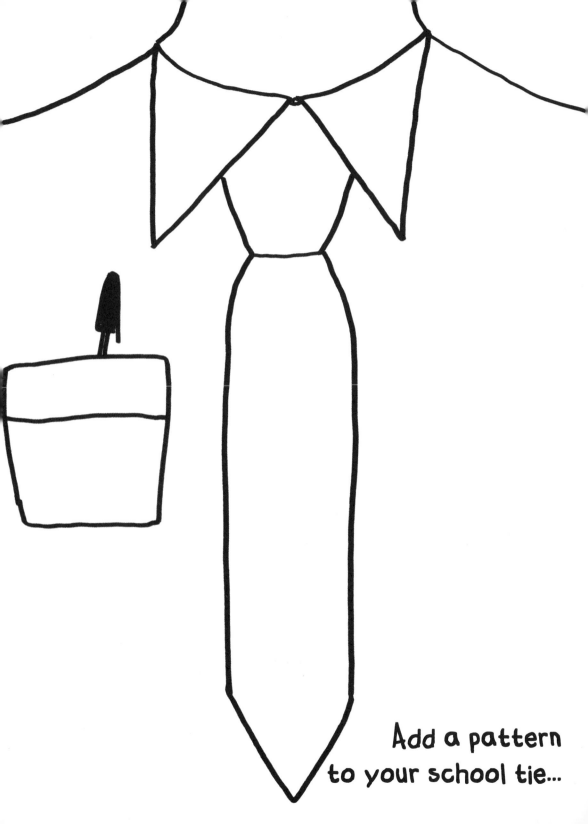

Add a pattern
to your school tie...

Give these teachers new hairstyles...

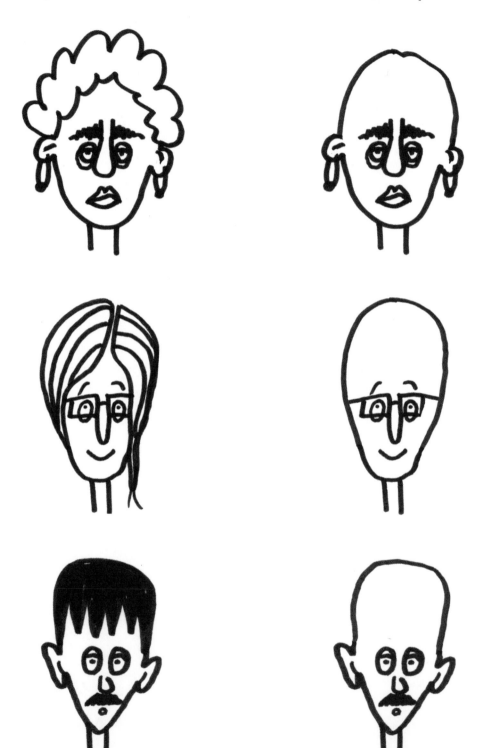

What huge creature has been
caught in the playground?

Fill in the sick note
From your mum...

Move your school to a completely new place...

The classroom is flooded!
What creatures are living in the water?

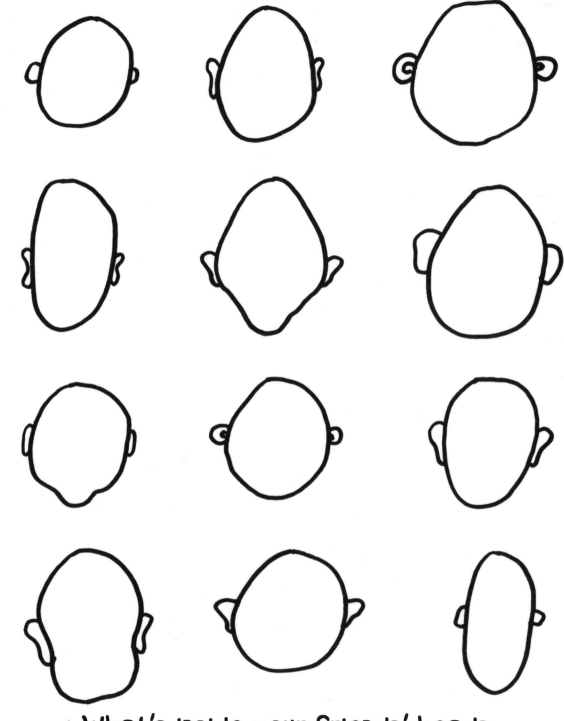

What's inside your friends' heads
where there brains should be?

Create your fantasy school dinner menu...

Menu

Stick a note on the teacher's back...

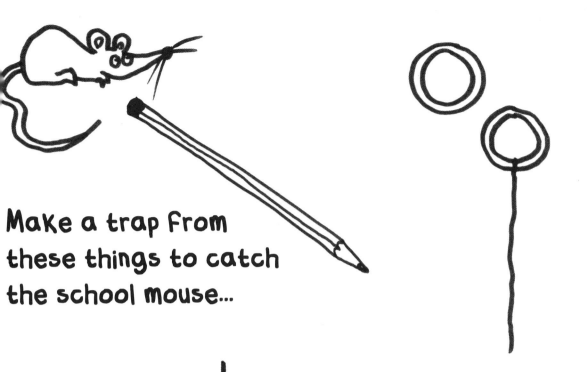

Make a trap from
these things to catch
the school mouse...

It's sports day.
Where are you in the race?

PROJECT 2:
Decorate
these cupcakes...

What is inside this teacher's head?

What ingredients are in today's school lunch?

Sarah is upset.

Draw something to cheer her up...

Now draw something to make her cry again...

The cleaners have forgotten to clean the classroom. Draw in all the mess!

PROJECT 3: Paint an amazing picture...

The class photo is being taken.
Fill in all the faces...

Design an exciting new cage
for the class hamster...

Decorate your schoolbag...

Who in the class has headlice?

Draw your worst lunch on the tray...

PROJECT 4: Fill in the map to create your very own country...

KEY

⌂ = my house

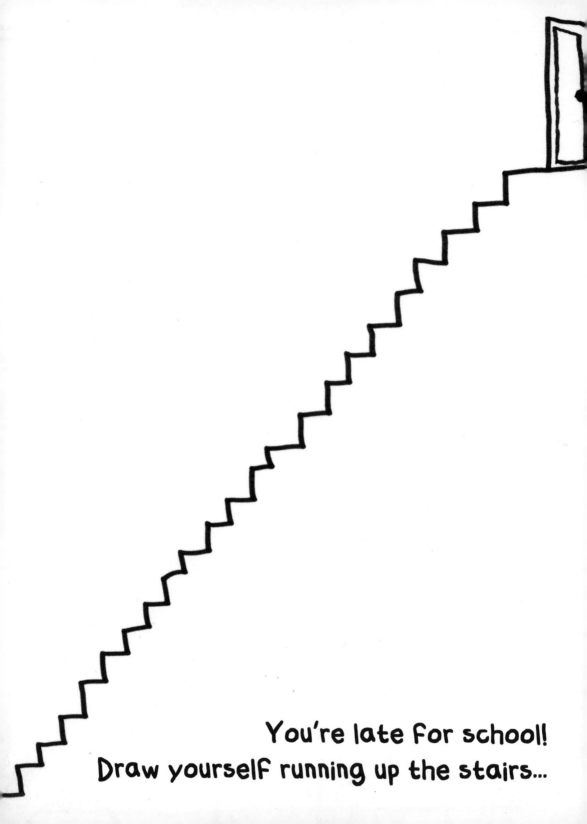

You're late for school!
Draw yourself running up the stairs...

What has Theo brought
to Show and Tell?

Design a new school uniform...

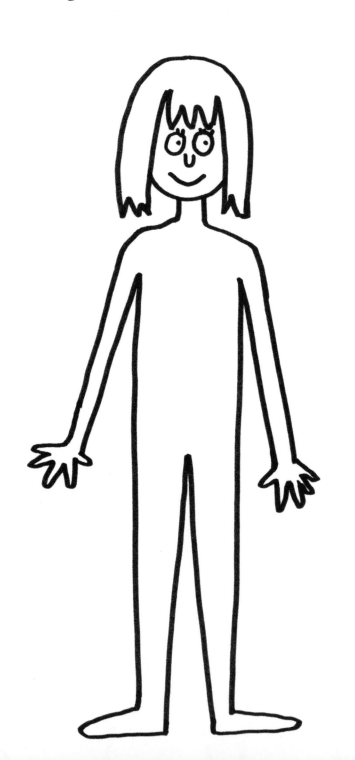

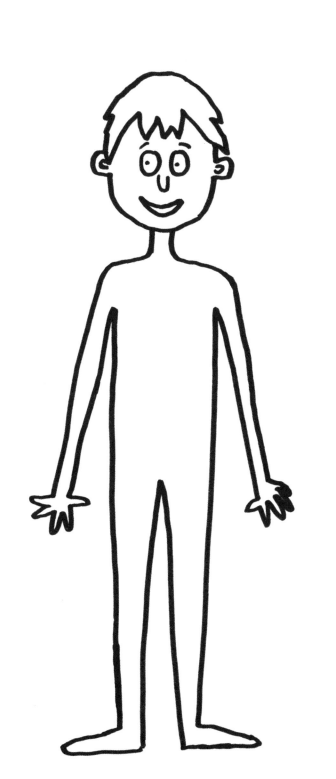

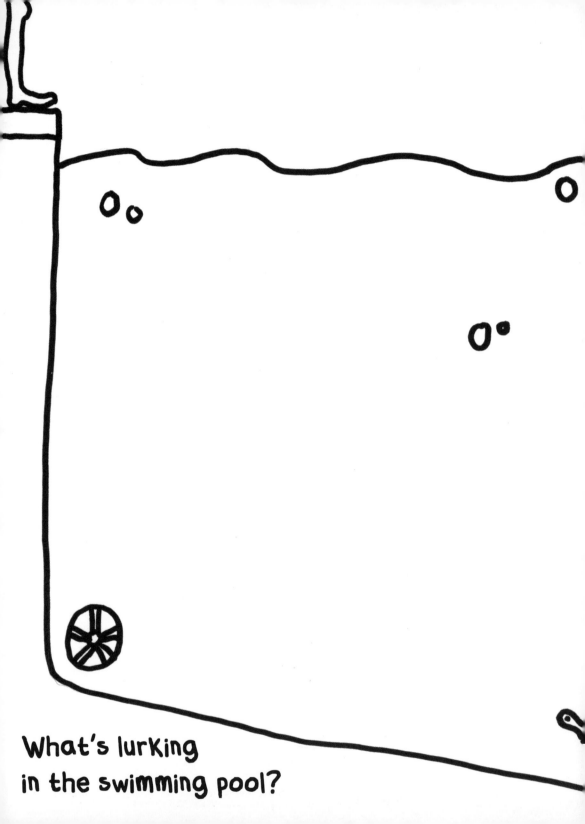

What's lurking
in the swimming pool?

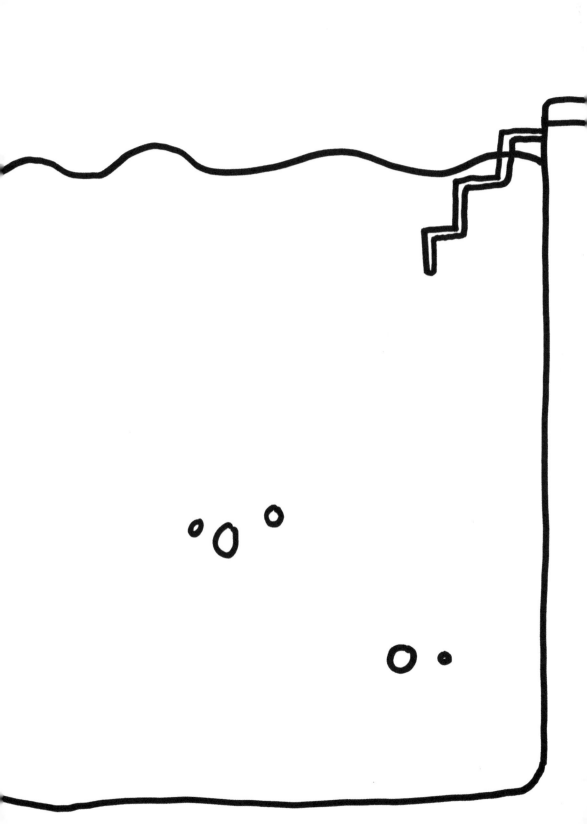

Make up your own multiple choice exam paper...

Examination Paper

1.
a)
b)
c)

☐
☐
☐

2.
a)
b)
c)

☐
☐
☐

3.
a)
b)
c)

☐
☐
☐

4.
a)
b)
c)

☐
☐
☐

The classroom has floated
out to sea! Add a sail and
anchor to turn it into a boat...

Use these parts to build your dream climbing-frame in the playground...

What type of plant is growing on the teacher's desk?

What has frightened these school children?

Draw lots of water squirting
from the drinking fountain...

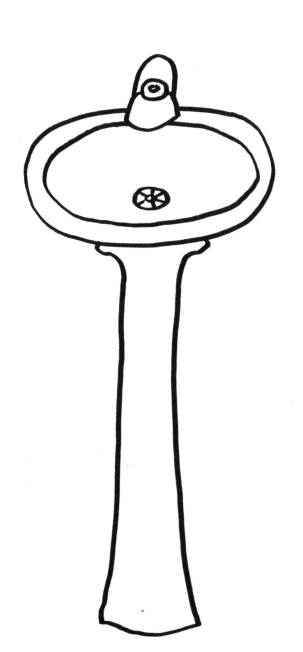

Give these children names...

PROJECT 5:
Turn these shapes
into real objects...

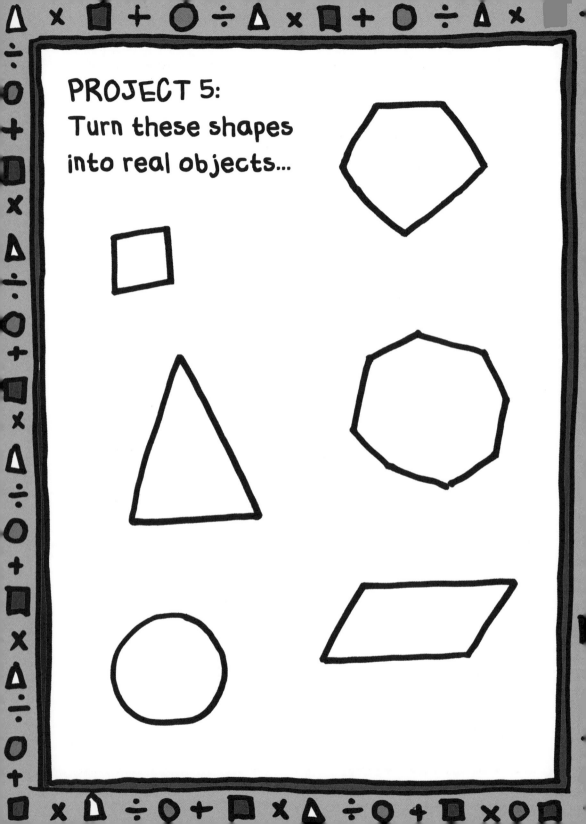

Hang your coat up on the peg...

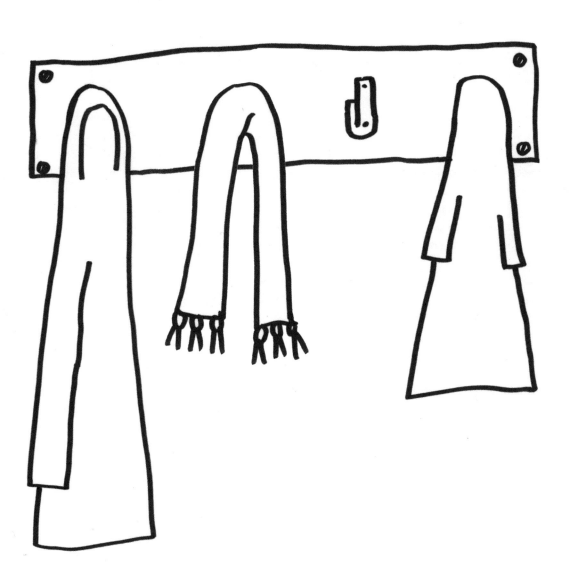

Make up a song for the school choir to sing...

Draw a mouse for your class computer –
a real mouse if you like!

Where is the Football?

Do some homework on your computer...

Draw the ink splattering
From this leaking pen...

Draw the faces for this gallery of teachers..

Miss Crumble

Mr McScruffy

Mr Jollywell

Mrs Twitter

Miss Prettywish

Mr Bristle

Mr Fuzzbody

Mrs Frostworth

Design a stall for the
school fair...

Sam has
chicken pox.
Draw on
the spots...

PROJECT 6: What will these things grow up to be?

What gift have you bought
for your teacher?

How many children
are jumping over the
skipping rope?

Draw yourself running out of the school gate...

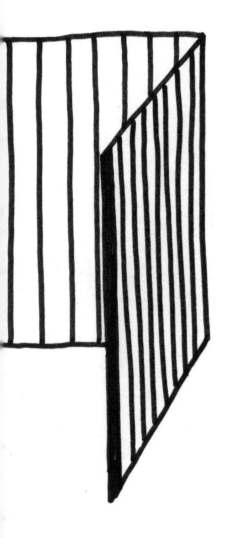

Doodle Report

Give yourself a mark out of ten for each of the following:

Drawing skills ☐

Brilliant ideas ☐

Neatness ☐

Colouring in ☐

Funny jokes ☐

Further comments . . . .

. . . .

. . . .

Signed: . . . .